GOLF FOR LEFTIES

Bill Burr

NTC/*Contemporary Publishing Group*

Library of Congress Cataloging-in-Publication Data

Burr, Bill
    Golf for Lefties / Bill Burr.
      p.   cm.
    ISBN 1-57028-129-7
    1. Swing (Golf)   2. Left- and right-handedness   I. Title.
    GV979.S9B87   1997
    796.352'3—dc21   97-24829
                                              CIP

Published by Masters Press
A division of NTC/Contemporary Publishing Group, Inc.
4255 West Touhy Avenue, Lincolnwood (Chicago), Illinois 60646-1975 U.S.A.
Copyright © 1997 by EPI (Eyelevel Products International)
Printed in the United States of America
International Standard Book Number: 1-57028-129-7
98 99 00 01 UG 20 19 18 17 16 15 14 13 12 11 10 9 8 7 6 5 4 3 2

TABLE OF CONTENTS

GOLF FOR LEFTIES

Credits:
Photos by J. Walker
Illustrations by Swing Meyer
Proofread by Pat Brady
Cover Design by Phil Velikan
Some text adapted from the book *The Biomechanics of
Power Golf* by Swing Meyer, and used with his permission.
Index adapted from the book *Youth Golf* by Cliff Schrock
and used with his permission.

1

TWO GOLF SWINGS:
TWO VASTLY DIFFERENT RESULTS

Good players "gather up" large amounts of energy by winding their major muscle groups: hips, thighs, chest, back and shoulders. All the muscles in the body's trunk.

Then, they transfer that gathered energy out to the arms, hands, clubhead and, ultimately, the ball. In the process, they turn the club into a whip and literally crack it. Through impact, their hips brake and the clubhead takes off like a rocket.

In all sports — and certainly golf is no exception — the athlete who can transfer

> *All I've got against it (golf) is that it takes you so far from the club house.*
>
> — *Eric Linklater*

maximum energy in the most efficient manner is probably going to be the winner.

To get a picture of this, imagine a Ferrari traveling at 125 miles an hour. It has great speed but zero acceleration. Now imagine that car hitting a brick wall. Anything sitting in the front seat is going to experience maximum energy transfer in the form of acceleration.

If we put an object on the roof of your car traveling at a more modest 55 miles an hour and offered you $100 if you could launch that object 50 yards down the road, what would you do? Would you slow down gradually...or would you hit the brakes HARD?

To achieve clubhead speed, good players involve major muscles. To achieve acceleration, they "brake" those muscles so the clubhead can fly. It's a basic law of physics: you stop...so something else can go. In the "braking" action, strong legs mean strong braking. You are the Ferrari. Your legs are the brick wall. The clubhead is the object in the front seat.

Computer analysis of place kickers reveals that strength in the planting leg is as important as the kicking leg. The kicker approaches the ball then plants his left leg so the kicking leg can "crack."

Golf acts as a corrective against sinful pride. I attribute the insane arrogance of the later Roman emperors almost entirely to the fact that, never having played golf, they never knew that strange chastening humility which is engendered by a topped chip shot.

— P.G. Wodehouse

Through impact, the good player disengages the gears so he can free wheel it. Get a picture in your mind of Jack Nicklaus' swing and you will see the epitome of this in action. Through impact, those huge thigh muscles come to a virtual stop and the clubhead cracks, like a whip.

The not-so-good player swings his hands and arms from his shoulder joints. At the top of the backswing, his energy tank is on "empty." To gather up energy in order to strike the ball, he has only two options: cast the club with the shoulders or with the hands.

Then, in a desperate effort to square the clubface and hit the ball, he uses the only body parts he can: his hands and arms. As opposed to letting energy transfer, the average golfer tries to "help it."

> *Your worst putt will be as close as your best chip.*
>
> *— Arnold Palmer*

To give you a picture of this swing, imagine somebody cutting a trail in tall grass using a scythe. Most people mis-hit shots because they have never trusted their swing to the major muscle groups. They want to control it with hands and arms.

Why is this so? Typically, the underachiever in golf perceives the sport as a hand/eye, hit-the-ball game. The target becomes the white sphere between their feet. "To hit that tiny ball," they think, "I better go after it with my hands and arms so I have 'control'."

The good player, when he or she is at the top of their game, transfers massive amounts of energy and the ball simply gets in

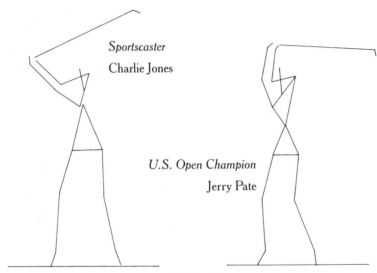

Sportscaster
Charlie Jones

U.S. Open Champion
Jerry Pate

At the Top

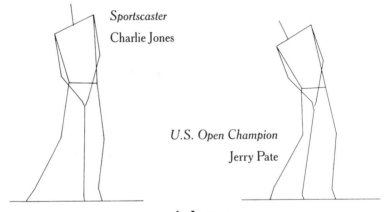

Sportscaster
Charlie Jones

U.S. Open Champion
Jerry Pate

At Impact

the path of that energy and is taken along for a ride out to the target.

One would imagine there is a huge difference between the golf swings of good and not-so-good players. Have a look at a digitization of sportscaster Charlie Jones and former U.S. Open Champion Jerry Pate on the opposite page.

The truth is, the difference in the two swings is measured in inches and split seconds. That's all. But...those inches and seconds translate to a wide variance in body and clubhead speed. Have a look at these numbers comparing the golf swings of touring professional Alan Tapie and an 18-handicapper:

	ALAN	18 HANDICAPPER	BIOMECHANICAL DIFFERENCE
Hip Speed	1.80 mph	1.25 mph	144%
Hand Speed	13.00 mph	8.80 mph	148%
Clubhead Speed	70.00 mph	46.50 mph	150%

The purpose of this book is to give you three concepts that will allow you to generate numbers more like Alan Tapie and less like the 18-handicapper.

The biomechanically sound golf swing has three qualities:

1. Structure

2. Linkage

3. Sequence

2
BUILDING A SOUND STRUCTURE

Imagine a quarterback under center ready to receive the ball. Can you see it? Picture John Elway barking the signals and setting his body, the crowd roaring in anticipation.

Now imagine a tennis player ready to receive serve. Can you see Steffi Graf shifting her weight side to side, ready to spring like a cat if need be? How about a third baseman getting set to move with the pitch...or a swimmer ready to dive with the sound of the gun?

These images reveal the athletic ready position for sports. Just before they "play," the athletes build a sound structure ready to transfer energy. To see how it looks in golf, look at the illustration on the previous page.

SET THE SPINE ANGLE

Our golfer has set a spine angle at address. He will maintain that angle going back and coming down. Only past impact will the angle and the structure come "up" to follow the flight of the ball.

> Golf is like faith: it is the substance of things hoped for, the evidence of things not seen.
>
> — Arnold Haultain

In the golf swings of weekenders, too often we see the angle destroyed. Lifting or dipping throws the club off plane and the shot off line.

STABILIZE AND ANCHOR THE BACKSWING

The left foot, left knee and left leg stabilize or anchor your backswing. When the backswing is stabilized, wobbling and swaying are eliminated. You then turn around a fixed axis.

Here again, we see the lower left quadrant of weekenders breaking down, resulting in a sway. Interestingly, sports in which throwing is important usually depend on a linear transfer of weight, not rotary. since you learned to throw a ball before you learned to swing a club, there is a good chance you brought this motion to the golf swing.

There are four other measurable qualities in the golfing structure:

1. Arms are straight

2. Club points to belt

3. Mind is focused

4. Weight is balanced

These points are illustrated on the next few pages.

◆ ◆ ◆ ◆ ◆

First, the arms are hanging straight down, relaxed.

Second, the club shaft is pointing at the belt line.

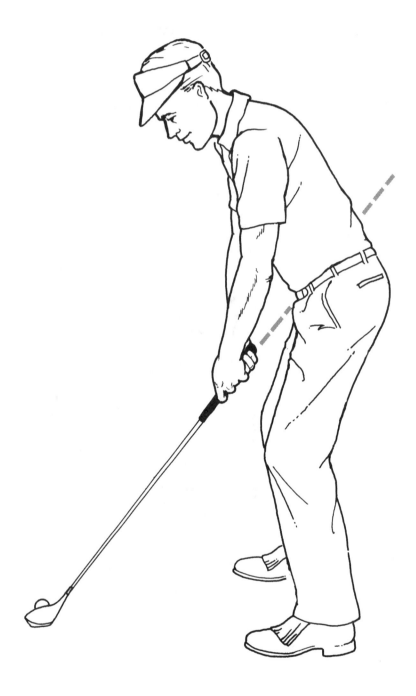

Third, the mind is focused on the target.

Fourth, the weight is balanced evenly between the feet.

Both feet are flat on the ground with the weight directly below where you tie your shoelaces.

There is one thing in this world that is dumber than playing golf. That is watching someone else play golf. What do you actually see? Thirty-seven guys in polyester slacks squinting at the sun. Doesn't that set your blood racing?

— *Peter Andrews*

To better understand the contribution of the ground, imagine a full swing standing in a canoe or on a sheet of ice with street shoes. In golf, we want motion, yes, but we also want to use feet and legs to stabilize the swing and keep us on the ground and in balance.

3

LINKING THE PARTS TOGETHER

In a connected golf swing, there are links that tie the swing together so it functions as a whole.

The links are as follows:

1. Torso to arms

2. Arms to hands

3. Hands to club

4. Club to ball

TORSO TO ARMS

The upper arms, particularly the left arm, rests snugly against the torso. When you can generate the feeling of the torso or trunk holding on to the arms, you'll have it.

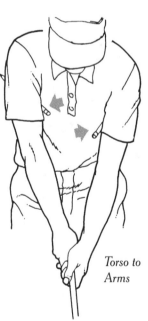

Torso to Arms

Since energy is being gathered by the major muscles and transferred to the arms, it stands to reason we need and want a connection between the two. Get the feeling of holding two pencils under each armpit...and feel the torso grabbing hold of the arms and the arms resting snugly against the torso.

They work together, never independently. It's like dancing. Arms and trunks together, back...and through. With rhythm and timing.

ARMS TO HANDS

The arms connect to the hands through the wrists. In our structure, we want the wrists relaxed. We want the arms hanging down with the wrists "low" in a semi-cocked position. As you turn back, this will allow the wrists to hinge upward.

Arms to Hands

HANDS TO CLUB: THE GRIP

Obviously the grip is the only physical contact with the club. Therefore a good grip is paramount in the building of a good golf swing. A bad grip equals a bad swing. Spend time on the building of a good grip, and the effort will pay dividends for all of your golfing days.

There are various ways to grip the club, the interlocking grip, the ten finger grip and the most popular of all, the overlapping (or Vardon) grip. The overlapping grip is the best grip for the majority of golfers, and is the one I recommend.

The grip should be taken with the right hand first. A good idea is to let your hands hang down from your side in a natural fashion. Let your fingertips point to the ground, place the club across your palm, and make sure that it runs across the hand from the middle of the right forefinger to a spot about three-quarters of an inch below the base of your little finger. Hold the club so that about $1/2$ inch extends beyond the heel pad of your right hand.

By not gripping the club right at the end of the grip, you will have greater control over your club during the swing. This little adjustment will help prevent loss of control at the top of the swing.

Grip pressure should be felt in the last three fingers of the right hand. Your grip should be firm enough to maintain control of the club. However, it should never be so tight as to strangle the club. You must be able to feel the clubhead as it works its way back and then down through the ball. All the fingers are closed around the grip. Your thumb should sit there just to the left of center on top of the shaft. The "V" that is formed between your thumb and forefinger should point toward your left shoulder.

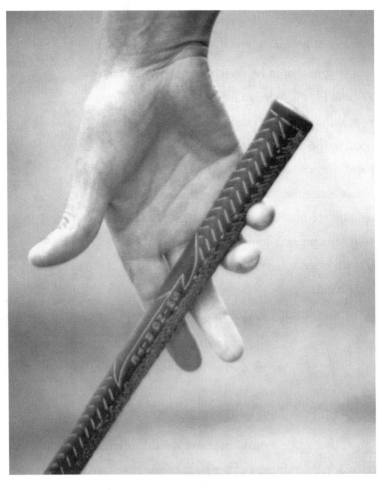

The club across the right hand.

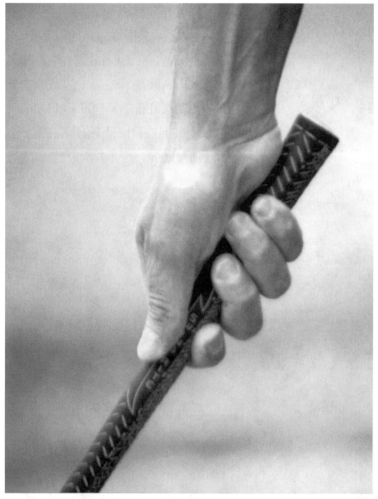

The right hand closed around the grip.

The best grip, one which will work effectively for a long, long time is one which is neutral in nature. The grip should never be too strong or too weak. When the right hand is properly in place, move the left hand into position by making sure the palm of your hand squarely faces the target line. The left hand grip is one

where the grip is placed primarily in the fingers. Think about lightly curling the fingers; this will create a natural channel for the grip to sit in. Here your left thumb should rest comfortably to the right of the shaft, and the "V" formed by the thumb and forefinger will point toward your left shoulder.

The club across the left hand.

The left hand closed around the grip

The right hand is largely responsible for the control of the clubface during the swing. However, the left hand is the one to supply the power. You should feel a little touch of pressure in your left thumb and forefinger and have the idea that it is the left hand that whips the clubhead through the ball. The reality is that the hands work together, but it helps to be aware of the important part your left hand plays in creating clubhead speed. It cannot be emphasized strongly enough, that the grip is the bedrock of a good golf swing. The hands must feel comfortable on the club, and they must work as a unit in order to control the clubhead — even at great speed. You may want to experiment with other grips, but the fact of the matter is that most of the tour players and most of the good amateur players prefer the overlapping or Vardon grip.

Both hands closed around the grip.

As you assume your grip and set up over the ball, you should be able to look down upon your completed grip and see at least two knuckles of the back of your right hand and the first knuckle on the back of your left. This will indicate to you that your grip is in a good

I've had a good day when I don't fall out of the cart...

— Buddy Hackett

position to return to the ball in the square relationship required for solid accurate ball striking. As noted, the hands are the mandatory ingredient for any golf swing to properly function at its best. "As you grip the club, so shall you swing" is a good thought to keep in mind.

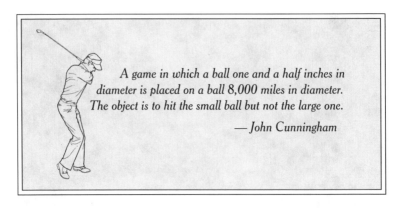

A game in which a ball one and a half inches in diameter is placed on a ball 8,000 miles in diameter. The object is to hit the small ball but not the large one.

— *John Cunningham*

Generally, if your tendency is to hook the ball, you have a grip which is too strong and your hands are turned too far to the left. To correct this, work at getting your hands back to the neutral position. If you are a slicer, you probably have a grip that is too weak and the hands are turned too far to the right. To correct a slice, give the hands opportunity to work from the neutral position. There is no need to add further difficulty to the golf swing.

CLUB TO BALL

For the driver, three-wood, five-wood and long iron shots — up to and including the four-iron — the best ball position is just opposite the right heel. This position will encourage a good clean strike and a ball flight that will bore through the air. With these clubs, the intent is to sweep the ball off the turf.

As you move through the middle irons (5-, 6- and 7-irons), the strike you want to produce will be a little different. You are attempting to contact the ball as you get to the very bottom of your swing arc, with the club traveling parallel to the ground after impact and only lightly brushing the ground after impact.

For these shots you will want to move the ball back about one inch in your stance.

For the short irons (8-, 9-, PW- and SW-), you will want to move the ball back in your stance about two inches. In other words, the clubhead is descending as it approaches the ball and that will encourage a golf stroke which will ensure that the ball is struck first. Then the turf will produce maximum backspin. This backspin is very desirable on approach shots to the green.

Practice your swing with these ball positions, find out where the best ball position is for your swing and work to make it efficient and trustworthy for your particular swing pattern.

4

ALIGNING BODY AND CLUB

Alignment is critical to the game of golf. If your alignment is off, your game is off. You will always be struggling to get the clubhead back square to the ball. The body must be aimed parallel to the target for all normal shots. A good grip and a trustworthy alignment procedure will make the shotmaking procedure much more consistent. Sometimes we forget that the idea is simply to get the clubhead back squarely and consistently to the golf ball.

> *If I had my way, any man guilty of golf would be ineligible for any office of trust in the United States.*
>
> — *H.L. Mencken*

Do not fall into the bad habit of aligning your body to the target. Always remember that the clubface is aimed at the target, but your body is aligned parallel to the clubface.

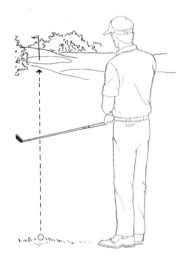

Do not fall into the bad habit of aligning your body to the target. Always remember that the club face is aimed at the target, but your body is aligned parallel to the clubface

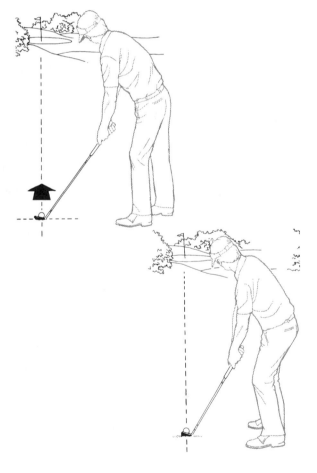

This means, in effect, that your body is aligned to the right of the intended target line. If your shots are finishing up to the left of your target, you should first check your alignment. Generally you will find that your aim has been to the left of the intended target. The tried and true way to check your alignment is very simple. You will see the touring professionals do this at every tournament, especially on the practice green. What you need to do, and should do, every time you practice is to lay a club down behind the ball in line with your target. Then place another club about six to eight inches outside the ball, exactly parallel to the first club. Finally move the club that is directly behind the ball and replace it inside the ball, parallel to the other club. These two clubs will serve two purposes as they train you to set up correctly to the ball. First, your body will sense the correct parallel position to the target line. Secondly, the clubface will be directed at the target. These procedures should be followed each time you go to the practice area and thus become second nature. The accuracy of your shots will be that much better.

Use a mirror to get the feel and look of these positions ingrained in your golf set-up. Remember your alignment procedure is critical to the improvement of your golf game. If the professionals feel that this alignment procedure is worth doing, then how much more important can it be for the average golfer? This may be the one secret to playing consistently good golf. Make sure that your feet, knees, hips and shoulders are aligned parallel to the target for all normal shots and watch your scores come down.

Many professional find that the method illustrated here is another good way of checking your alignment.

POSTURE

This is where the overall position of your body comes into the swing. The posture has a great deal of influence on the way you will swing a golf club, so it makes sense that you should do everything you can to ensure that you can swing the way you want. The correct posture will place your body in a position that will allow your arms to swing freely on the correct plane, body to stabilize, balance to be maintained, and your weight to be shifted correctly during the swing. One factor which is often overlooked in relation to good posture is whether or not your clubs are the correct length for you. If your clubs are correctly fitted, you will have less trouble finding the proper spine angle. As you ground your club, flex your knees and balance your body, the correctly fitted clubs will aid your posture and your set-up to the ball.

A good foundation will provide the stability required for maintaining good posture. This foundation can be established as you take your stance. A normal walking step is about the right width for most golfers and should result in a stance that is slightly wider than your shoulders. The weight should feel centered over the balls of your feet — never on the toes or heels. The toes and heels are deadly wreckers of balance and rhythm.

One area that is critical to the set-up has to do with how you bend or tilt toward the ball. You must bend from the hips but at the same time push back slightly with your hips toward your heels. The position should feel comfortable — a springboard, athletic sensation. You are poised, relaxed and ready to move. This is another area of the swing where you might want to use a mirror to check your position. Sometimes what we think we are doing and what we are doing are two vastly different things. It is best to visually check your position if it all possible. It is also important to retain the angle of your spine throughout the swing.

With the body in good position, the arms are free to hang down from the shoulders. This will place your hands in a position that will be underneath your chin. The arms will be comfortably

I play with friends, but we don't play friendly games.

— Ben Hogan

extended with no tension or stiffness. The right arm will feel more in control of the swing and will play a major role in its width. The left arm will be softer, slightly lower than the right and ready to fold correctly on the backswing.

The club you are using will determine the distance that you will stand from the ball. You will strive to maintain the same posture, but adjust to accommodate the length of the club shaft you are using. The angle at which each club sits has been designed to give you the best results with that particular club, so make certain that the club sits properly at address. Quite naturally, you will stand a little further away from the ball with your driver than you would with a pitching iron. There is a reason for the varying lies and lofts which manufacturers design into their clubs. Learn to use this to your advantage. If in doubt, check with your golf professional or a competent club fitter. Your ball striking may benefit from an adjustment to your clubs.

5

SEQUENCE

Once the structure is set up...linked...and aimed, the only remaining task is to keep things in the proper sequence so maximum energy is transmitted to the club head.

The reason most golfers "hack" is because they have never been taught how to solve two problems:

1. How to hit a ball in front of them.

2. How to hit a ball on the ground.

If the ball is in front of them, somehow the club must be swung around their bodies like a merry-go-round. If the ball is on the ground, then somehow the club must be swung up and down like a Ferris

> *I deny allegations by Bob Hope that during my last game I hit an eagle, a birdie, an elk and a moose.*
>
> *— Gerald R. Ford*

wheel. But, how much "around" and how much "up and down"?

In this sequence section, we will show you how to solve this "bi-directional" problem.

Remember, the golf swing you see is an illusion. The backswing and through swing you see is the net result or effect of something else that's happening that you cannot see! We are going to show you the "something else."

THE FULL SWING

This is the area of the golf game where every player wants to shine. Everyone wants to hit the big drive, the big three-wood into the long par fours, and the par fives.

Where does it all begin?

Right back at the basics of grip, stance, posture and alignment.

Develop sound fundamentals and the game of golf is made so much more manageable. This is not to say that all swings are alike. We have only to look at the PGA tour to see how varied are the swings of the top players in the world.

However, that said, these top players all have one thing in common. That one thing is the routing of the club head down, and through the ball. A good thought to have is this, that you want your clubhead to arrive at the ball as close to the address position as is possible. You will not be able reproduce the address position exactly, because the address position is static, and the impact position is one of movement. The fact remains however, that the concentrated effort to reproduce the address position will result in much better golf shots. After all, since this is the goal of the tournament player, why not make it your goal as well.

The development of this game plan will give you the freedom to fully concentrate on the target. "Pipeline" Moe Norman, the renowned legend of golf, and one of the best ball strikers the game has ever known, always concentrates on where he wants the ball to go. He can do this because he has perfected his swing to the point where he has absolute trust in what he can do with it. Moe never struggles with the mechanics of his swing during a round of golf; his only thought is how does he want to shape this specific shot.

All golfers, to be successful, need to get to this point with their game, to know their swing strengths, the method, and the ball flight that will produce the best results on a consistent basis.

The pay is great, and the only way you can get hurt playing golf is by getting struck by lightning.

— Ted Williams

Obviously, the top notch players of the world do not waste time trying to be some one else and watch the tournaments played each week on television. No two players look alike; they all work to their own strength. Every good golfer will benefit from following this example. The full golf swing is a movement that starts from address, moves to as close to parallel at the top, as your physical abilities will allow, then continues back to impact, on through to the follow through position, with the club across the shoulders, and down the back.

Take away

Pivot

On Plane

Hinge

All of this should be accomplished with smooth timing, rhythm, and balance to produce the proper result. Too many golfers speed up on the backswing, cut it short on the backswing, speed the clubhead down from the top position, stop the swing at the ball, and fail to complete the follow through.

The result is a shot that lacks power, direction, and will generally sail off into the hated slice, or into a duck hook. This type of swing is usually a result of negative thinking, because the golfer is trying to avoid doing something wrong. Much better if the concentration is directed towards doing what is right. Visualize the shot, the swing you want to produce. Be positive. Make adjustments slowly, because if your golf game suffers from a chronic slice, it cannot be corrected in one session.

The uglier a man's legs are, the better he plays golf. It's almost a law.

— H.G. Wells

It will take time to make the change. Work on the idea that slow and sure changes will last for the long run. Quick fixes are not going to bring long term solutions, which is really what we want. It is especially important that the full swing never be thought of as anything but a swing. What it is not is a series of movements; it is a swing. Once you get that concept firmly mbedded in your mind you are ready to improve your golfing experience.

I guess there is nothing that will get your mind off everything like golf will. I have never been depressed enough to take up the game, but they say you can get so sore at yourself that you forget to hate your enemies.

— Will Rogers

THE TAKE AWAY

The take away is the all important start to the backswing. If we can get all the moving parts moving away together, then we have a much better chance of producing a swing that will generate optimum results.

The club, hands, arms, shoulders and torso should all move away from the ball in a one-piece take away. Again, all the great players start their swing in this fashion. Why not imitate their

A good one-piece take-away

proven methods? It stands to reason, that if these important units do not work together, then they will work in opposition to each other, resulting in confusion, and poor swing results.

Now the head may shift a little, as you make the initial move away from the ball. You must avoid the trap of moving too much, because this will cause the body to move off the ball too. Not very many players are skilled enough to get all these moving parts back to the address position, so the idea is to keep the backswing from causing too much movement off the starting position. One way to ensure that movement is minimal is to concentrate on the back of the ball. It is amazing what a simple focus key can do to improve our full swing shots. The back of the ball is where we plan to have the club strike the golf ball, so why not look there?

You can do worse than take a page from the technique of Jack Nicklaus. He turns his chin slightly away from the target as he begins his backswing, and he keeps his chin up off his chest. This gives his shoulders room to turn. You ought to try this in your own swing, and make it part of your routine. Don't overdo it, just a gentle turn to the left will do.

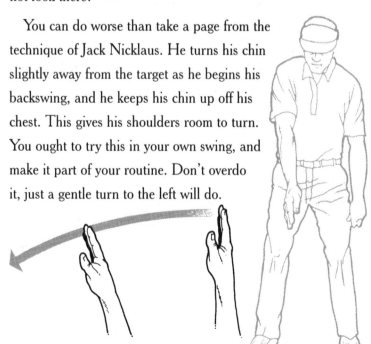

Correct take away line

A one-piece take away will give your swing a wonderful opportunity to gather itself into a total and complete swing through the ball. Herky-jerky "bits and pieces" swings are doomed from the start, and will never be consistent and pleasurable things to take you around the golf course. Work on a smooth, one-piece take away during your practice sessions, and reap the rewards on the course.

You must swing the driver, and fairway woods, with some authority in order to produce distance, and good direction.

If your basic fundamentals are good then this should be no problem, but if there are any weaknesses in your routine then they will show up very quickly. To develop the smooth, balanced coordinated swing needed you might want to make some swings with your feet close together; this will force you to swing smoothly, and to stay in balance. Not too many golfers want to do this exercise, but if you will spend a few minutes, at each practice session, swinging with your feet together the benefits will make it very much worthwhile. For one thing, you will soon learn what your optimum swing speed is, and learning to swing at this speed will be of great benefit to your golfing progress.

THE WRISTS

You start the backswing, correctly, and get to the point where the arms, and club shaft, are parallel with the target line. Here you will find that the wrists will have to break, or cock, in order for the club to get back as close to horizontal as possible. At this cocking, or breaking point, in the wrist be careful that firm control is maintained over this action. Looseness here will affect the rest of the swing.

The wrist cock: an important aspect of the backswing.

The hips come into play on the backswing, and although they turn, they do not turn as much as the shoulders do. The best ratio of hip turn is about 50% of the shoulder turn. If you can turn your shoulders 90 degrees, the hips should be turned to about 45 degrees. Unless you are making a conscious effort to turn the hips more than 45 degrees (not recommended), you should not have to think too much about the shoulder and hip relationship. It is much better to focus upon the flex in your knees. Try to keep that flex throughout the entire swing, especially the flex in the left leg. You should feel the weight positioned to the left side as your backswing winds around your left leg. The right hip is turned around the right knee, which should point at the ground just a touch behind the ball, no collapsing of the knee. The big key is to retain the flex in the left knee all the way through the swing. Make your turn around the knee. A stable knee will prevent any swaying off the ball to the left. The weight should feel as though it is on your left heel. The final backswing movement occurs in your right heel. It either comes off the ground, or rolls over very slightly. Your degree of flexibility will determine which route you take.

The swing plane is vital to the overall success of the swing, and only comes about if the arms and the shoulders turn in harmony. If you swing only with your arms, but do not turn your shoulders, then your swing will not be on plane. So, whether you are swinging a driver, or a nine-iron, the swing plane is correct if you train your arms and your shoulders to work in unison. It is perfectly normal to have a flatter swing plane with a driver than you do with a nine-iron. The longer shaft and flatter lie of the

The sequence for the backswing is shoulders, hips, knees, feet.

WRONG: shoulders opening!

RIGHT: shoulders still fully turned at start.

Hands and arms come straight down.

driver will produce a more rounded swing. A vital key to a consistent swing plane is the maintaining of the spine angle. Your shotmaking will be so much better if you can set up properly to the ball, and then maintain the same spine angle throughout.

The backswing starts out as a one-piece take away, all the parts working together. As the swing progresses the shoulders assume a more active role, and play a large part in turning your body around your left knee to the top of the swing. The sequence is shoulders, hips, knees, feet.

THE DOWNSWING

Here is where the golfer faces the toughest part of the golf swing. You can be trained to reach the top of the swing in pretty good fashion, but if the downswing is not started correctly the entire swing motion is lost. This may sound rather difficult to accomplish, however it can be done, and here is the best way to make the downswing work for you. Give all your attention to the elements of the swing which were used in getting to the top of your backswing. Try to have the reverse happen on the way down to the impact position. The right heel was the last part of the body to move on the way back, so let it be the first thing to move down to its original position. If you do this, and you must practice these moves so that they will occur naturally on the course, then the rest of the swing elements will, if you let them, follow the natural sequence.

Follow this sequence and the swing will be assured of a much better chance of succeeding. Right heel back to the position it occupied at address; once this happens then the right knee and right hip will return to their starting positions. This move will assist in aligning your feet and hips on the correct ball target line.

The knees and hips move the upper body. It will start its movement through the swinging of the arms, and clubhead, down toward the ball, then on through the target line to a full finish. If done correctly the clubhead will approach the ball from an inside out target line.

Always remember that the shoulders come into the swing picture last. The shoulders action is a result of the legs, hips, and arms. The early use of the shoulders is one of the most disastrous moves in golf, and leads to all kinds of problems. The use of the shoulders, too soon in the swing, will cause problems, such as coming over the top. Coming over the top means that the clubface will approach the ball from the outside in, resulting in sliced, or pulled shots, neither of which is pretty to see. The arms have to be given enough room to work around the body. If the shoulders spin out too soon then there is no place for the arms to go, but out and away from the body.

Remember to get this sequence of things on the way down: heel, knees, hips, arms, shoulders. Now you do not want to be thinking of all of these moves when you are out on the golf course. Practice on the driving range, or play a few holes, late in the evening, when the course is not very busy. Check with your teaching professional, to ensure that you do have these fundamentals of a good swing properly ingrained into your procedure. It cannot be stressed enough that you do not work through your swing on the course. If you practice correctly, then a good swing comes "naturally," and your main concern should be the target.

When you swing through the ball, make sure you do just that.

The golf swing is one continuous motion, composed of a backswing and a continuing swing through the ball, down the target line, and into a full follow through.

The ball gets in the way of the clubhead, as it is traveling at its greatest speed, en route to the target. There is no slowing up at impact; the momentum of the clubhead must be at its greatest to ensure solid contact, and the optimum results.

Remembering the correct order of the swing, at all stages, is the key to success. Coming down your body will rotate, and continue to rotate, not slide, after the ball is struck and the right knee will hold its position. As the club passes waist high, your tummy should be facing the target. Your swing will continue with the arms and shoulders continuing until the club is over the right shoulder, to the right of your right ear. This should produce a mirror image of the position you were in at the top of the backswing. The weight should feel predominately on the right heel and the toe of the left foot.

All of this may sound complicated, but is in reality the product of good fundamentals, and if you make a good swing through impact, it should occur in a natural fashion.

Again, the way to get the feel for all of this is to spend time on the practice range. Make small swings, over and over again, so that you develop a feel for how the swing feels, and works. On the course you just do it, but it will be much easier for you if the time has been dedicated to the practice area. It cannot be said too often, if you want to improve, you must spend the time to learn the proper technique.

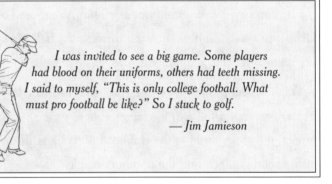

I was invited to see a big game. Some players had blood on their uniforms, others had teeth missing. I said to myself, "This is only college football. What must pro football be like?" So I stuck to golf.

— Jim Jamieson

Get a feel for the clubhead, where it is at each part of the swing, use two clubs for a warm up, and you will sense the location of the clubhead. Use a weighted club. You can make one from an old club. Just add lead tape and swing it repeatedly, this will give you a very good sense of where the clubhead is at all times. It will also give your golfing muscles a good workout, so you can kill two birds with the one stone. The weighted club will also encourage you to swing smoothly, because in order to sense the clubhead you must swing smoothly, and with good rhythm and timing.

The Feel and the Illusion

Through impact, you may feel that your hips are going toward first base. And you may feel that the hands and arms are going toward third base. The net effect? You shot rockets out to center field. Perfect.

The next time you see Tiger Woods play, watch with this thought in mind. You will see the classic example.

The average player often tries to steer the ball to center field. When you steer, you lose coil and you lose centrifugal force. The result is a weak grounder to the pitcher.

The on-plane swing, then, is the net effect of a bi-directional move: the hips pivoting and left forearm extending down through impact like a lever.

The weekend golfer tends to sabotage his shot by shooting his left hip up in the air and sliding. Analyzation and comparison of the swings of Jack Nicklaus and President Gerald Ford showed a dramatic difference. Nicklaus rotated around a fixed axis. The President swayed going back and slid going forward.

When you sway or slide, it becomes a hands and arms effort. What you get are big chops, huge divots and skied tee shots.

When the left forearm fails to extend downward through and past impact, what you get are topped, low runners. We see them most often with long irons and fairway woods.

Go back to the structure for a moment. The spine angle we set allowed you to pivot or rotate. And the way we linked the club to your hands allowed you to hinge, un-hinge through impact, then re-hinge to a finish.

More than anything else, the motion through impact is a free-wheel, almost out of control feeling. We have solved the "mystery" of the swing by balancing a rotational pivot with a vertical hinge to produce a desired end result: solid contact with a ball that is in front of you and on the ground.

When a player is hot, the pivot and the hinge are in balance. When the player's not, the pivot and hinge are out of balance. Today's tour players are so good even small imbalances spell the difference between making the cut and cashing a check...or heading down the road Friday night. What happens to the golf club in a balanced golf swing? For openers, you are able to use your arms and the club as a whip to crack through impact, compressing the ball. Mechanically speaking, you have as follows:

1. Since the hands and arms come straight down, you have a stressed shaft and a lagging club head...just like a whip to be cracked. (See illustrations 1 and 2 on following page)

2. An on-plane shaft as a result of a balance between pivot and hinge giving you a correct angle of attack. (See illustration 3 on preceding page)

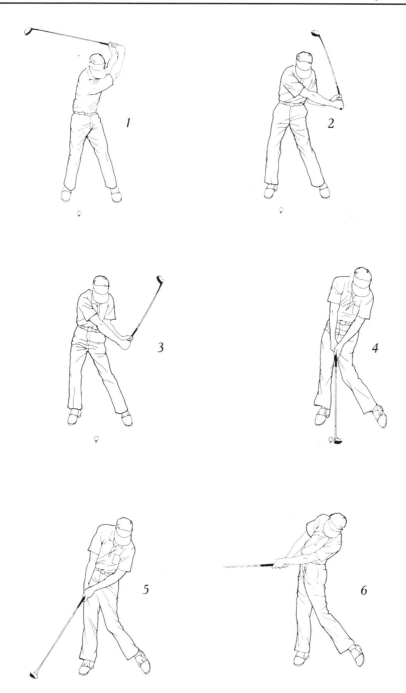

3. Just before impact, the hips brake...and your stored up energy is transferred through the arms, wrists, hand and club shaft out to the clubhead. The hips "stop" so the clubhead can "go." This is the freewheel. (See illustrations 3, 4, 5 and 6)

4. A flat right wrist through impact for clubface control. (See illustration 4)

Obviously, you will tend to feel what you focus on. As you develop, look for the following senses:

♦ Light arms

♦ Heavy club head

♦ Heavy feet

♦ Stressed shaft

♦ Soft hands

♦ Clubhead lag

These are all good sensations.

So, you start it with your center of gravity. You keep it going with a balanced pivot and hinge. And you repeat it because your mind understands the task...and your body swings in compliance with the laws of physics.

In the backswing, the upper body is the leader. The lower body is reactive.

In the forward swing, the lower body is the leader and the upper body is reactive. No shoulders, please. It's hips and arms straight down — left forearm extending down through the ball — to a finish.

Energy comes from big muscles: hips, thighs and trunk. It is the uncoiling or rotating of these parts that causes the left forearm angle to catapult to a straight position through impact.

Just before impact, the rotation slows so the arm and club can go. Imagine a shot putter. He spins around, generating energy. Then, the right foot plants, the hips stop, and the shot goes. That's Newtonian physics at work.

Having logged literally thousands of lessons with golfers at every skill level, all golf instructors can point to the #1 problem of weekend golfers:

> Show me a man who is a good loser and I'll show you a man who is playing golf with his boss.
>
> — Anonymous

they try to get in there with the hands and help it. This destroys the shot. It destroys everything.

When you trust your swing to the laws of physics, you build a sound, repeating swing.

Over time, you build in so much freedom — physical and mental — that you feel the club swinging you. The game becomes a joy.

Now that we've discussed the elements of a good golf swing — lets see how we can put those elements to use in the various swings we use during a round of golf.

6
THE DRIVER

The one club which all golfers want to use to its fullest is the driver. This is the club which produces the most satisfying feeling for most golfers. What golfer doesn't like to see his tee shot zoom off the tee, and straight down the fairway, out there in good position for the approach shot to the green.

It is a tremendous feeling to hear the crack of the clubhead, as it meets the ball squarely, and solidly.

> *Golf matches are not won on the fairways or greens. They are won on the tee — the first tee.*
> *— Bobby Riggs*

Having said that, you must understand that the most important element of the drive is accuracy. Length is good, but accurate length is better.

The stance is a very important part of the driver swing; if your stance is too narrow you will lack the stability to make a full attacking swing at the ball. If too wide, you will inhibit the shoulders from making a good shoulder turn.

Either of these faults will lead to a loss of power. So always work at having your stance about the same width as your shoulders; this width will vary for other clubs, but it is best to have a consistent setup for the driver.

The take away is the crucial move in the driver swing. The old adage 'low and slow' is still the best advice when it comes to describing the first move back with the driver. There is a sense of being very smooth with the take away: no jerking, no rushing, no quick pick-up of the clubhead.

To obtain the fullest turn, away from the ball, will depend on how flexible you are, so it always pays dividends to spend some time working on stretching exercises. This is the reason Sam Snead, well into his eighties, continues to play golf with such skill. Sam is renowned for his flexibility, and he works at maintaining this flexibility through exercise. You should work at this aspect of the game as well.

The ideal turn will have your back facing the target. A good swing thought is "left pocket back." This move will ensure that the hips are turned as far as required, and will also bring the shoulders around to the best position. The productive driver swing is based upon good fundamentals. Good execution of those fundamentals will result in a full coil at the top, arms high, back to the target. From this powerful position you are set to unload a swing, with power, that will produce consistent results.

The productive driver swing is based upon good fundamentals. Good execution of those fundamentals will result in a full coil at the top, arms high, back to the target.

Coming back down to the ball we want to remember the fact that the right leg and hip will move toward the ball laterally. Getting back to the position they were in at address, but, and this is important, not beyond that point. We do not want an out of control lateral slide. The correct lateral move will bring the right arm downwards to the ball on the correct inside out path.

When the lower body leads the swing, then a lag of the hands, and the clubface, will result in what is sometimes referred to as a delayed hit. The hit is not really delayed, but the clubhead and the hands should be the last things to come into play, with the release creating tremendous speed and power through the hitting area.

With the impact position in mind, you should strive to arrive at the address position as closely as possible.

When you have reached impact, and the ball is on the way to the target, you have no further control over where the ball is going to go. However, a good follow through position is an excellent indicator of a good swing. For one thing, if you finish in a good position, chances are the rest of your swing will generally be very good. Never try to 'fake' the finish of your golf swing; it will serve no useful purpose, and only delude you in your attempts to achieve good swing habits. A good finish will happen if all of the preceding motions have followed the fundamentals.

'Flowing' is an excellent way to describe the attributes of a full swing with the driver. Be a "practicer" on the range, and a player out on the course.

7
SWINGING WITH THE IRONS

With the irons the goal becomes much more precise than with
the woods. It always pays to be accurate, but with the irons the
pay off can be
wonderful for
your scoring.

> Give me my golf clubs, fresh air and a beautiful
> partner, and you can keep my golf clubs and the
> fresh air.
>
> — Jack Benny

When you get
within range of
the green, it is imperative to be able to hit your iron shots at the
flag. This is where the low scoring players excel.

The one area which will help you in your iron play, is to
remember that a good full body turn is a very dependable way to
ensure that your swing will be compact, and powerful. Too often
the average player will hesitate to turn away from the ball with the
upper body, and will rely on the arms to direct the clubhead to the
ball, and to the target. Usually, this is a recipe for missed shots.

The hardest shot is a mashie at ninety yards from the green, where the ball has to be played against an oak tree, bounces back into a sandtrap, hits a stone, bounces on the green and then rolls into the cup. That shot is so difficult I have only made it once.

— Zeppo Marx

At address, align your body square to the target and distribute your weight evenly between your feet. Check to make sure that your right arm and the club shaft form a straight line, and from this position you will form the radius of the swing. Get the swing off to a good start by turning the hips and knees in a smooth rotation away from the target.

Keep the take away smooth, and wide, and this will help you to make the correct shoulder turn. Get the right shoulder under your chin, with your back and the club shaft facing the target. This will load the backswing for a powerful attack upon the ball. The ideal is to reach a 90-degree turn with the shoulders, and about 45-degrees with the hips. This will coil the large muscles of the hips and back. As this power is released in a natural uncoiling of the backswing, the clubhead will travel on a correct, and powerful line through the ball.

If it is not possible for you to turn 90-degrees with your shoulders, make the effort to turn as far as you comfortably can. This will bring the greatest degree of success to your shotmaking.

As you coil to the top of the backswing, the weight is transferred to the left side, supported by the left leg, especially the left
knee. The downswing requires that you get that weight back to
the right side; this is very important. Failure to do this will result
in the dreaded fault of fire and fall back, with a very poor and
weak shot generally the result. To achieve the correct result try to
think about having the arms, legs, and the body working back
through the ball, and on out to the target.

Here is an idea that will assist you to achieve this feeling of
everything working together. Imagine that the butt end of the
club is pulled towards the ball as the club starts its downward
motion to the ball. A swing thought such as this is all we need,
in many cases to help produce consistent reliable shots. This
idea will also go a long way toward helping you to stay behind
the ball at impact. Transfer the weight to the right side, follow
through in good balance, and the task will be well accomplished.
Failure to shift the weight onto the right side can cause difficulty
in getting the clubhead back to the ball, blocking your proper
attack upon the ball. If this sounds like a problem you might
have, then think hip and shoulder turn, and release of the body
coil with a strong hip and leg action, through the downswing.

8

THE SHORT GAME

So, the round of golf is over, and you store your clubs until the next game. As you are relaxing with your golfing partners, the one question that always seems to come up is "what did you shoot?" Not "How far was your drive on the long par five?" or "How many putts did you take?" but "What did you shoot?" Learn a lesson from this, and remember that the only thing that matters, in golf, is the score.

It's just the old fashioned pool hall moved outdoors, but with no chairs around the walls.

— Mark Twain

This brings us to the short game, where the real game can begin. Without a good short game the scores will just not be as low as they can be, and as they should be.

Miss a drive, and you can recover, miss a fairway shot and you may still be able to recover, but miss a pitch shot, a chip shot, or a putt and there is no recovery. The shot is lost and goes onto the score card.

So let me encourage you to place a great deal of emphasis on the short game. Practice all of the shots from 100 yards in, and watch your scores come down.

Here are some of the ways to save shots in that critical area of the game, from 100 yards in. This is the area where you will be hitting about 70% of your shots in a typical game of golf. So, why not do all you can to improve this part of your golf game?

What is important, with regard to your thinking, is that when you play

I just loosen my girdle and let the ball have it.

— Babe Zaharias

these shots, strength and brute force are not required. What is required is rhythm, and balance. Indeed, without these two components no one can hope to be a proficient short game player. So, work on these two items, and follow the tips which follow, work at least 50% of your practice time on the short game, and reap the rewards of a solid short game.

The closer you get to the hole the less power you need to get the ball to your target, so you have to create smaller swings. For example, the pitch shot will require more clubhead speed, thus you will have to transfer weight, and you will have to use your wrists during this swing. Contrast this with the chip shot, which is played mostly with the arms and hands, rather like a long putt.

One of the first things you must learn about your short game, is this: How far do you hit your wedge on a consistent basis? It is amazing how many golfers neglect to obtain this information. Then are often confused during a game, to the point that they either come up short, or are too long, with their approach shots. One of the goals of your practice is to determine exactly how far you hit with certain clubs. This knowledge alone could save you valuable strokes in every round.

Once you have determined that you hit the ball 90 yards with your wedge, as an example, then do what all good players do, try to get your approach shots into that range all the time. Good players do not hit to within 90 yards on one hole, then 60 yards on another. No, they play to their strength, and are striving to be at that comfortable range as much as they can. This frees them up for attacking the flag more aggressively, or for making the most judicious approach to the hole.

One caution here is that you should not take unnecessary chances. Always leave yourself a margin for error; the objective is to get the ball on to the green. When you get a wedge in your hands remember that this is a scoring shot that you are going to execute. This is not the club for obtaining distance; the stories of 150-yard wedge shots are usually nothing more than that. Think score with the wedge.

The wedge shot requires nothing more than a three-quarter swing. The best way to obtain the proper wedge swing starts right at the address position.

Alignment is the same as your normal set-up. Hips, shoulders, and club should all be parallel to the target line. However your feet should be a little open, (aligned right) and a little bit closer than you would place them for a mid-iron. This will restrict your left side in turning your body away from the ball, thus a shorter swing. The ball position should be just a little bit inside the right heel, and your hands ahead of the ball. Don't make the mistake of pushing your hands too far forward. That would only de-loft the club, and you need the loft of your wedge to obtain the best results. Grip the club lightly, but with firmness. The weight should be a little more to the right side. About a 60/40 distribution, in favor of the right side, should be about the correct split. This will assist you to bring the club down through the ball in the correct path through impact.

Always think smooth. Always think tempo. You are hitting within yourself, so no need to rush the swing. The wrists will begin to break just about where your hands have moved to a point opposite your left knee. The clubhead weight will tell you when this should occur.

Your objective is to maintain the smoothness all the way through the swing. You will not need to worry, too much, about your weight shift on this type of shot. You are not trying to crack out a drive; this is a scoring shot. Swinging back in balance is an excellent way to obtain the proper position, and you will not need to apply a lot of conscious thought to the process.

Coming down into the ball your objective is to concentrate on remaining smooth as you change direction.

The way to do this is to focus on your feet, let them dictate the rhythm of your forward movement. Transfer the weight from your left foot to your right foot, and stay light on your feet. The arms should swing freely, and follow the lead of your feet and legs. Shifting the weight smoothly, without jerking, is very important in the production of an effective short swing. A smooth effort will bring the clubhead smoothly through impact, and result in a decent shot most of the time.

The pitching wedge, or nine-iron, will get the ball airborne for you; that's why these clubs are designed with a higher degree of loft. Let the club do the work.

There is absolutely no need to flick the club at the ball in order to get it airborne. Such unnecessary action will only destroy the purpose of the club, and result in inconsistency of flight and direction. Always, always remember that you are trying to hit this shot the same distance every time.

Your follow through should mirror your backswing, and should maintain the same pace, tempo, and length as your backswing. In other words, do not swing through any farther than you swung back. Finish in balance.

For a shorter pitch shot, as you work closer to the green, the way you control the distance is in the use of a swing which is smaller in its arc. The worst thing you can do is attempt to hit the shot, with the full wedge swing, at a slower pace. It is almost impossible to hit a solid shot when the clubhead is decelerating. You will never achieve consistency with such a method.

Instead, maintain the same rhythm and tempo used for the full wedge shot, but do not swing so far back, or through. Keep the clubhead accelerating. Your alignment remains the same as for the full pitch shot, parallel to the target line, but your stance should open up a little more, and be placed a little closer together. Should you have to play an extremely high shot, you might want to open the clubface and shoulders just a touch, but normally you would keep them square to the target.

This opening of the stance, along with the narrower stance, will naturally restrict your backswing, so learn to work within those restrictions, and do not overextend your swing. Sometimes you may have to improvise with your grip by gripping down on the club. This can be the case when you are "in between" clubs. Don't be afraid to use your imagination; it can often result in saving a shot around the green.

CHIP SHOTS

Here is the shot that is basically controlled by the hands and arms. You could consider any shot within 20-25 yards of the green to be a chip shot. When you are hitting the chip shot, using only the arms and hands, you will not be hitting the ball very far. Force is not required — it is much more important to control the shot with a balanced rhythmic motion, with swing length dictating how far the shot will travel. The chip shot is also an area of the game where imagination plays a great part in determining the success of the outcome.

Don't fall into the trap of relying upon one club for all of your chip shots. As you approach your shot look over the situation carefully, and make the decision about which club you will use based upon the information you glean from this survey of the upcoming shot. Based upon this information you should then make the proper club selection, and proceed to get the ball as close to the hole as possible. The clubs which you should consider for chip shots would include the sand wedge, pitching wedge, nine-iron, eight-iron, and seven-iron. The purpose is to master one swing with different clubs for all of the chip shots, rather than different swings with one club, which is much too difficult to master. So, work to polish the one swing with different clubs, use your imagination, and the short game will be your best friend in the lowering of your score. Here are some of the things to remember with your chip shot method.

Again, the stance must be narrowed. The weight now shifts

Golf is a sport whose secret is to hit the ball hard, straight, and not too often.

— Anonymous

to your right foot. This alteration will assist you in making the slight downward movement through the ball that will aid in producing the crisp contact with the ball. The chip shot is a simple golf shot, so keep it that way, don't overthink it, be decisive, and swing smoothly at all times. Do not jerk the club in a fast motion, and then decelerate on the way through; this is an instant recipe for disaster. One more thing, keep the head quiet — no peeking too soon.

Good chipping will depend upon how much time you are willing to spend at the practice area. Quality practice time will pay big dividends out on the course. Get to know your chipping clubs, how far you hit them and which one is best for the shot required.

Here are some guidelines for you to work with.

Seven-iron — use this club for a shot which will require one third of the shot to be in the air, and the other two thirds traveling on the ground.

Nine iron — generally will be used for shots that fall within the range of fifty percent in the air, and fifty percent on the ground.

Pitching wedge — this club will be used to carry the ball further in the air, and less on the ground. About seventy percent in the air, and thirty percent along the ground.

Maintain a degree of flexibility with these shots. The foregoing are good general rules to follow, but again these are shots where you must let your imagination come into play.

Concentrate on the distance you want the ball to travel, rather than on the direction. When you look at the target visualize a five foot corridor. This is fairly easy to do, so then all you have to concern yourself with is the distance. Always practice in this fashion, and you will soon be much more proficient with your chipping game.

Except in very unusual circumstances, you want to land the ball on the putting surface, and let it run to the hole. You will find that this procedure will give you a much more predictable outcome. If the ball hits on the fringe then there is a greater possibility of getting a bad bounce.

Always pick a spot where you want the ball to land. This is much more productive than trying to land the ball at the hole, resulting in a shot that travels too far.

When you practice your chipping, be sure to do so with the various clubs you use for the short game. If you spend all of your time working with the one club, then you will shortchange yourself, and miss the scoring opportunities which will come your way out on the course.

> *No matter what happens – never give up a hole...*
> *In tossing in your cards after a bad beginning you also*
> *undermine your whole game, because to quit between*
> *tee and green is more habit forming than drinking a*
> *highball before breakfast.*
>
> — *Sam Snead*

Another aspect of the short game which you need to have in your arsenal is the matter of gripping the respective clubs at the proper position on the grip. Usually you would hold the seven-iron at the bottom of the grip, the nine-iron halfway up; and the sand wedge as you would for any normal shot. Again, these are guidelines, and you should experiment with your grip to ensure that you are comfortable with your procedure, and that you are getting maximum results from your chipping.

Having said all of this, always remember that golf is not quite a predictable game. Not every shot will fall into neat little categories, therefore the imagination will come into play, a great deal, on the chip shot and the pitch shot. You will be faced, from time to time, with shots that need to be hit higher, or lower, from a divot, or from the rough. Here are some of the methods you can use to get you out of these difficult spots.

For a shot that you want to get up quickly, the best way to accomplish this is by adjusting your address position. The high shot will be easier to obtain if you learn to open your clubface. The added loft will flight the ball higher, and help it to land softly. This is one shot where you also open the body, including the shoulders, to the right. Keep your hands level with the ball, not ahead as you would with a normal shot. These adjustments will give you all the height you can expect with your wedge. One other thing; do not quit on the shot, keep the head steady, and you will obtain a good result, every time.

The low shot also requires some minor adjustments. You will need to position the ball back in your stance. Keep the hands forward, without overdoing it. This will de-loft the club, and get you into the proper position for hitting a low shot. The shot is a fairly steep angle of attack down into the ball – more of a punch shot. Again, don't quit on the shot, stay down until the ball is well on its way.

All of the advice in the world will not do you a bit of good, unless you are prepared to spend time at the practice area. You must be willing to work with the short game. Spend, at least, as much time as you do trying to launch killer drives into the next county. Golf is a scoring game, and the good players have a good short game.

An essential part of a good short game is knowing how to recover from the shot which goes astray, and ends up in a sand bunker. This happens to the best players in the world – just watch them during the big tournaments on television, you will see plenty of action from the bunkers. We are not automatic machines; we are human beings, and the potential to err is always present during a round of golf. But, you know what? The top professionals in the world, if they miss a shot, are very happy if they end up in a bunker. This is because they know this is one of the easiest shots they face in the game of golf. It is easier than a three-foot putt!

If you will follow the following guidelines, you too will be able to approach your bunker shots with a confidence that will make an "up and down" a sure thing every time.

When you find yourself in a bunker here is what you should do.

Start by shuffling your feet into the sand, but don't get too deep, just enough to give you a solid foundation, and to give you a feel for the type of sand you are in.

This will also serve to lower the arc of your swing, essential to aiding you to hit the sand behind the ball. This is one shot where you do not have to hit the golf ball, just the sand behind the ball. What could be easier than this?

You must open the clubface, and your entire body, for this

shot because you want to get height on the shot, up and on to the green. Place your hands level with the ball, and have the ball positioned opposite your right heel. When you settle in for this shot, and feel comfortable, then open the face of your club, and always do that before you take your grip.

Always open the face of the club, then take your grip. It is a fatal error if you fan the club open after you take your grip. This will cause the clubface to return to square at impact, often resulting in the thin skulled screamer that runs across the green, into another bunker, adding another shot to your score. One other thing which I recommend doing is lowering your right shoulder during your set-up. You will find that this little adjustment will assist you in getting under the ball.

Factor into your shot that the ball will fly to the left of where you aim. So you must allow for that, and aim right of where you want the ball to land. Let your swing follow your body set-up. Don't try to swing the club too far to the inside; this will negate your preparation adjustments.

The Swing

Many times we make the swing much too complicated. We do better when we can spend time, on the mechanical part of the game, during serious practice sessions, and then when we get into a bunker operate from a position of trust. The game is much easier when we learn to trust our swing.

You will make a normal swing along your body lines, and as you are set up in an open position this will guarantee an out-to-in shape to the shot. This is a result of the way you have set up to the ball. From here all you have to concentrate on is making a

The uncomplicated swing

smooth swing. The worst thing you can do in a bunker situation is to become anxious. Relax, this is one of the easiest shots in the game of golf. Aim to hit the sand, not the ball. About one to two inches behind is a good rule of thumb. Don't quit on the shot! The sand will carry the ball onto the green.

There will be times when the bunkers will not be in perfect condition. So make sure that your bunker practice includes shots from less than perfect lies. You will be ready for whatever situation you may face. To be prepared, you must spend time in the practice bunker.

9
PUTTING

Here is where all top class golfers shine. They can putt extremely well. They work hard on the practice green. When they move out to the course, the only thing they concern themselves with is speed, and the line. The mechanical part is all taken care of.

The grip is a somewhat individual thing, but there are some guidelines, and here is what most of the top players in the world consider to be the best type of grip.

Most of these players strive for a palm-to-palm hand position on the club – a

...the reason the pro tells you to keep your head down is so you can't see him laughing.

— Phyllis Diller

neutral position, in other words. They have learned, through trial and error, that it is not good to have the hands "fighting" each other. Let them work in harmony. In assuming the grip on the club it pays to have a grip which feels comfortable. If you are always twitching and moving the hands to get this comfortable feeling, then it will be worth your time to devote some effort to achieving a grip which is comfortable, one which produces good results, and which becomes second nature to you when you have the putter in your hand. Once you obtain a comfortable, effective grip, stick with it, and this will become part of your consistent routine.

The most popular grip in use today is the 'reverse-overlap,' a simple adaptation of the famous Vardon grip – the right forefinger is positioned outside the fingers of the left hand. The thumbs should rest on the top of the grip, this will promote a solid, square alignment, and go a long way toward putting the ball along the correct line to the hole.

The reverse-overlap grip supports the back of the right wrist, and provides a firm wrist action through the ball.

Because the right wrist is prevented from breaking down, the stroke will keep the putterhead moving low to the ground. This is the action you need, in order to produce consistent, solid contact with the ball. The hands need to work in unison, just as they do with a full swing. However, the right hand will be the hand which acts as the directional controller, and the left hand will be the hand supplying the feel, or touch, to the putt.

It may be that you want to try other grips, just as you probably try other putters. Even the tour players are always searching for the ideal putter, looking for the magic club which will give them "the edge." Believe me, no such club exists. The "secret" to putting, as with all other parts of the game, is simply dedication and hard work. Once you have found the formula which works for you, stick with it. If it works consistently over a period of time, and then goes sour for a while, check out your routine. Something you are doing is different, so find out what it is, and correct the flaw. Don't fall into the trap of trying to rebuild the wheel. The game of golf is such a mind game, and the mind comes into play more with putting than in any other part of the game. Perhaps because we know that the shots on the putting green can never be recovered, we may miss the green, or the fairway, and be able to recover, but not so with a missed putt.

The rewards for spending time on the practice green are beyond estimate. A confident putter is the match of any golfer he meets. Here are a few more steps you can build into your putting stroke, in order to be an efficient roller of the ball on the green.

Use a grip that is not too tight, and not too loose. You want to retain the feel of the putterhead as you stroke the ball.

A grip that is sensitive to the clubhead, the ball, the green conditions will prove to be the most dependable in the long term.

With regard to ball position, I feel the ball should be placed somewhere between the center of your stance and the right heel. This permits you to see the line to the hole. Because the ball is positioned forward in your stance, you will promote an upward brushing type of stroke through the ball, and toward the cup. Playing the ball too far back in your stance will cause the ball to 'hop' as it travels away from the putter. Not a very consistent way to putt.

It cannot be emphasized enough that you must have your eyes properly 'sighted' over the ball, and the target line. If the target line, and your sight line, are not in sync, then the results of your putting are never going to be as good as they ought to be. The information you feed, through your eyes, to your body, play a very important role in

> If there is any larceny in a man, golf will bring it out.
>
> — Paul Gallico

determining how well you are going to putt. In the world of computers, the terminology, "garbage in, garbage out" applies very well to the place of the eyes in the putting game.

Check your eye position regularly. Make sure you are correctly positioned, and you will be a better putter.

From a square address position, it will be much easier for you to work your swing toward the hole. My feeling is that open stances, and closed stances, add a unneeded element to the putting stroke. It is much easier to set up square, on a consistent basis, than from the open or shut positions. The part of your body which influence the putting stroke the most are the shoulders, and that is why I believe the shoulders must be square to the intended target line.

The putting stroke is essentially a pendulum action, and for a pendulum to function properly it must hang straight down. Think about the pendulum on a grandfather clock: it would never operate properly, unless it was hanging straight down. This is the position which allows the clock pendulum to operate freely. It will also allow your putting stroke to operate most effectively.

Resist the impulse to crouch over the ball. Crouching will only restrict your swing. Instead, you should assume a position which will allow your shoulders, and arms, to swing freely. A cramped, crouched position will only restrict your shoulders, and arms, from doing their job, and will also lead to a more "wristy" action – not a dependable way to putt.

By standing correctly you will see the line of the putt much better, and you can follow the line by swiveling your head, rather than lifting it. Lifting the head to see the line makes it very difficult to keep your body aligned correctly, because the lifting motion will pull your entire body out of position.

With a good grip and a good set-up, you are ready to put a great roll on the ball, and the way to do that is by the use of the shoulders. The shoulders are what sets the pendulum in motion, and you control the shot with how far you let the pendulum move back, and through. With practice you will be able to maintain the triangle, formed by the shoulders, and arms, throughout the swing. The shoulders will rock back and forth, the same motion as you would use in rocking a baby in your arms. Smooth motion back, smooth motion through the ball, on out to the cup. These actions will assist you to keep the putterhead low to the ground, which is where it should be.

Tests prove that the best roll is put on the ball when it is struck in the middle, or just slightly below center. Line up your practice putts with the printing on the ball facing the hole. Then watch the ball as it travels toward the hole, if the printing is turning over, end to end, then you will have excellent feedback regarding how well you are stroking the ball.

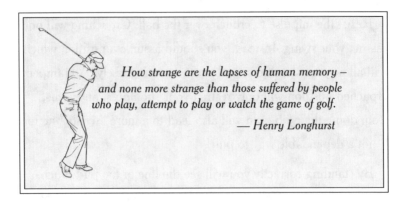

*How strange are the lapses of human memory —
and none more strange than those suffered by people
who play, attempt to play or watch the game of golf.*

— *Henry Longhurst*

The head of the putter will be straight back, and straight through, but, and this is very important, this will be only on the shorter putts, up to and including those of six feet. However, on the longer putts it is impossible to keep the putter going straight back, and straight through. The rules of geometry dictate that the longer strokes will require the putter to move inside the target line. So don't try to do the impossible – the stroke will not be effective if you try to force the putterhead to stay square to the target.

As with all other parts of your game, the need to practice is never more important than with your putting. Golfers tend to forget that fifty percent of the game takes place on the green. This area of the game deserves at least fifty percent of our practice time. Use the practice green at your course as much as you can.

Develop drills that will aid you in becoming a consistent putter. Stand over those three-footers with the same confidence that you have on the putting green, and you will be a better scorer.

The imagination plays a great part in a successful round of golf. So never hesitate to imagine "the shot" that will get you out of trouble, back in the fairway, onto the green, or close to the hole. The greatest players in the world do this. You can see them improvise shots at every tournament. Standard operating procedure will not always be the answer to a particular situation, so think your way out of the problem, determine the best solution, and execute it to the best of your abilities. It is often better to "take your lumps," with the shot at hand, than to try and pull off the shot of the century. Plan ahead, and you will be able to cut your losses, and move on to the next hole with minimum damage.

10
Drills

These drills, of course, are for the practice range or home practice. They are designed to help your mind develop understanding and your body the appropriate sensory feels.

When you play, go play. Hit shots to a target and get it in the hole as soon as possible. Remember, there are two games: "golf" and "golf swing." On the course, play "golf." Play "golf swing" somewhere else.

> *It is impossible to imagine Goethe or Beethoven being good at billiards or golf.*
>
> *— H.L. Mencken*

Finally, golf is a game, and a game is meant to be a thing of pleasure. Make sure you enjoy your round of golf, and the rewards of that mind-set will spill over into your game, with the result that you will become a better player.

Free arm swing drill

Set up. Then raise your right heel so you are on your right toes, like a twinkle toe. Then take a swing. Sense the free arm swing. Sense the hands and wrists hinging up and down. From the top, get a feel of the hands and arms coming straight down in a narrow, tight arc. Feel the arms, too, "packing in," close to the body. This is a great drill.

FLAT RIGHT WRIST DRILL

Hold the book against your forearm and take a swing. Through impact, sense a flat right wrist. Sense that wrist arched and going towards first base. Sense the hips rotating toward third. Can you see the shot rocketing over the center field fence? Can you feel there is no breakdown of the right wrist? Good.

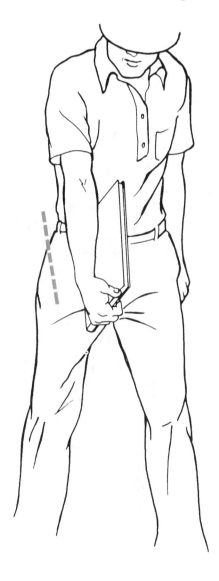

Rotational drill

Feel and sense the pivot. The trunk and shoulders sweep the club back, the hips bring it through. Rotate the club on a level plane, horizontal to the ground. Through the swing the club remains level with the toe in the air. Can you sense shoulders back, hips through? Upper body takes it back. Lower body brings it down and through.

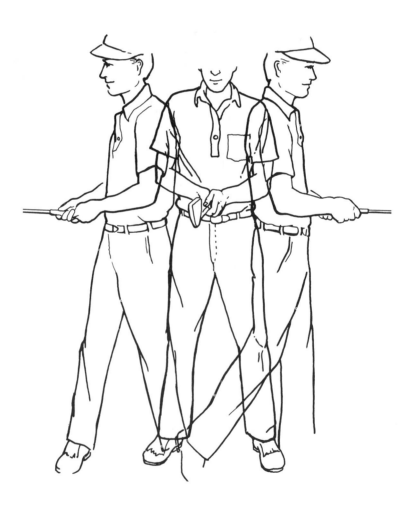

Take Away Drill

I'll give you $100 if you can unlodge the tee marker and take it back. What would you do? Pick it up with hands and arms? Uh uh. You'd recruit legs, thighs, hips, stomach, back and shoulders and then rotate them around a fixed axis. What a perfect take away! Sense relaxed hands and arms. Remember, your balance point starts the turn.

Impact drill

I'll give you $100 as well if you can unlodge the tee marker. What would you do? You'd recruit the same body parts as you did in the take away drill and try to snap the shaft. Sense the hips rotating and the right forearm extended down. Feel a flat right wrist.

GRAVITY DRILL

At the top of the backswing, feel the hips starting to move and initiate the forward swing. What causes the hands and arms to come straight down? Gravity. The upper body is now reacting to the lower body. Don't use any upper body part to help it. You'll cast or throw the club off line, dissipating energy in a premature release.

11

GLOSSARY OF TERMS

Ace: Another name for a hole in one.

Address: Posture a golfer assumes just prior to swinging.

Airmail: Struck ball that flies over the putting green.

Albatross: Another name for a double eagle.

All square: Tied match between two opposing sides.

> *Golf is played by twenty million mature American men whose wives think they were out having fun.*
> — *Jim Bishop*

Amateur: Someone who plays without accepting prize money or other compensation.

Approach: Shot played to the putting green.

Apron: Short-cut grass surrounding the putting green.

Away: Golfer farthest from the hole; on the fairway or green, this person plays first.

Back door: Ball entering the hole by curling around on the far side.

Back nine: Final nine holes in an 18-hole round; also called the "in nine."

Backspin: Reverse spin put on the ball at impact that helps it stop quickly on the putting green.

Backswing: Portion of the swing, starting at address to the top of the swing.

Bail-out areas: Places where the golfer can safely play to avoid trouble on the course.

Ball mark: Indentation made when the ball strikes the putting green.

Banana ball: Ball flight that curves sharply from right to left.

Best ball: Playing format involving teams in which the best individual score among team members counts toward the final total. (Also known as better ball.)

Birdie: Score on a hole one stroke less than par.

Bite: Similar to backspin; how well the ball stops upon hitting the putting green.

Blade: (1) Putter characterized by a thin clubhead; (2) Hitting shot less than flush.

Blast: Shot played from a bunker when the ball is partially buried.

Blind hole: Hole in which the fairway or green is hidden from the golfer's view; players hit blind shots to the fairway or green.

Bogey: Score on a hole one stroke more than par.

Break: Movement the ball makes on the putting green due to the green's curvature and slopes. The player must allow for break to putt the ball in the hole. (Also called borrow.)

Bump and run shot: Possible when the putting green is open in front; player hits a low shot that lands short of and rolls onto the green.

Bunker: Depression in the fairway, rough or near the green, either grass or filled with sand from which the golfer must play if his ball lands there. (Also called a sand trap.)

Buried lie: Ball is partially or completely covered in a sand bunker.

Bye: Exempt from playing in the first round of a match-play tournament.

Caddie: Person who carries a golfer's bag of clubs during a round and gives advice on club selection and shot strategy.

If you watch the game, it's fun. If you play it, it's recreation. If you work at it, it's golf.
— Bob Hope

Carry: Amount of land a ball needs to clear to reach a targeted area.

Cartpath: Usually paved, a narrow road through the course designed for use by motorized carts.

Cavity-back irons: Irons with weight removed from the back of the clubhead and distributed around the clubface perimeter; designed for players who often miss the center of the clubface.

Chili-dip: Similar to a fat shot in which a high-lofted club digs into the turf and moves the ball a few feet.

Chipping: Any of a variety of short shots played around the green.

Close lie: Ball sitting directly on top on the ground with no grass supporting it.

Clubbing: Helping a golfer select the correct club to play a shot.

Clubface: Grooved portion of the clubhead that makes contact with the ball.

Collar: Short-cut grass area surrounding the putting green.

Course rating: Varies from course to course; the score a 0-handicap player would shoot from a certain set of tees. The more difficult the course, the higher the couse rating.

Crosshanded: Unconventional grip style that puts the right hand below the left for a left-handed player, the left below the right for a right-handed player.

Crosswind: Wind that blows left to right or right to left as the golfer faces the putting green.

Dew-sweeper: Mis-hit shot that rolls along the ground.

Divot: Section of the turf removed from the ground by the clubhead during the shot.

Dogleg: Bent L-shaped hole, usually a par-4, that bends left or right after the driving area.

Dormie: Match-play term; a player is dormie when he leads his opponent by the same number of holes left to play.

Double bogey: Score on a hole two strokes more than par.

Double eagle: Score on a hole three strokes less than par.

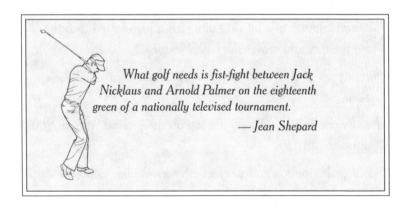

What golf needs is fist-fight between Jack Nicklaus and Arnold Palmer on the eighteenth green of a nationally televised tournament.

— *Jean Shepard*

Down: Trailing in a match.

Drive: First shot played off the tee; usually with a driver.

Driving iron: Most often a long iron, such as a 1-iron, used to hit the ball off the tee for accuracy.

Duck hook: Ball flight that curves sharply from left to right.

Duffer: Nickname for a high-handicap player.

Eagle: Score on a hole two strokes less than par.

Explosion shot: Same as a blast shot; hitting a buried ball out of a bunker.

Fade: Ball flight that gradually curves from right to left.

Fairway: Most expansive part of a hole; it's the short-cut grass area that is the intended route from tee to putting green.

Fat: Hitting the turf first behind the ball and then the ball; drastically reducing ball distance.

Fellow competitor: In a stroke-play tournament, the relationship between players.

Flat stick: Another name for putter.

Flat swing: Player's swing that is more horizontal than normal.

Flagstick: Consisting of a pole and flag, the flagstick is placed in the hole to indicate the hole's location on the green.

Flyer: Ball hit from the rough that has little spin to stop quickly on the putting green and thus rolls more than usual.

Flub: Mis-hit shot that is similar to a fat shot.

Followthrough: Completion of the swing.

"Fore!": Warning cry intended to alert players in danger of being hit by a ball.

Forecaddie: Person stationed in the rough near the driving area who marks where errant drives finish.

Forward press: Slight movement of the knee or hands that triggers the start of the backswing.

Forward swing: Portion of the swing from top of the swing to followthrough.

Four ball: Match in which two golfers play their best ball againt the best ball of the other two players.

Foursome: (1) Group of four golfers playing together; (2)

> *Every time I have the urge to play golf, I lie down until the urge passes.*
> *— Sam Levenson*

Competition in which two-man teams play against each other in an alternate-shot format.

Fringe: Closely cut grass immediately surrounding the putting green.

Frog hair: See fringe.

Front nine: First nine holes in an 18-hole round; also called the "out nine."

Gimme: Putt of such short length that it is conceded by a golfer's playing partners; a violation of the Rules of Golf.

Grain: Direction the grass on the putting green lies, affecting the break of the ball.

Green fee: Cost to play a round of golf.

Greenies: Betting game awarded on par 3s to the player closest to the hole with his tee shot.

Greenkeeper: Head superintendent of the grounds crew.

Grip: (1) Placing the hands on the club in preparation to swing; (2) Rubber or leather put on the club for the golfer to hold the club.

Grooves: Scoring lines on the clubface that help spin and control the ball.

Gross score: Player's score without the use of handicap strokes.

Grounding the club: During address, letting the clubhead touch the ground behind the ball.

Half/halved: In match play, used to describe a hole or match that ends in a tie.

Handicap: Number of strokes a golfer receives to equalize competition between poor (high-numbered handicaps) and better (low-numbered) players.

Hanging lie: Ball situated on a sharp downslope.

Hardpan: Hardened ground, usually without grass.

Headwind: Wind coming into the golfer.

Heel and toe weighting: Club construction method that distributes weight around the perimeter of the clubhead so mis-hit shots are not adversely affected as much.

Heeled shot: Shot hit off the heel of the club; there is a substantial loss in distance.

High handicapper: Usually a beginner; a golfer who receives a high number of handicap strokes, such as 30 or more.

High side: Area above the hole on a sloping putting green.

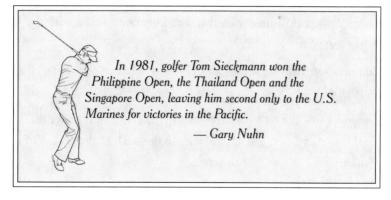

In 1981, golfer Tom Sieckmann won the Philippine Open, the Thailand Open and the Singapore Open, leaving him second only to the U.S. Marines for victories in the Pacific.

— *Gary Nuhn*

Hole: Lined, round opening on the putting green that is four inches wide and must be four inches deep; also called the cup.

Hole high: Ball that comes to rest, either right or left, level with the hole on the green or to the sides.

Hole-in-one: tee shot that finishes in the hole.

Holed out: Ball that falls below the level surface of the hole.

Honor: Hitting first on the tee; determined by a coin flip or blind draw on the first tee, by lowest score the rest of the round.

Hood: Holding the club so the toe of the clubface is ahead of the heel, decreasing the loft of the club.

Hook: Ball flight that sharply curves from left to right.

Imbedded lie: Ball that imbeds in wet or muddy turf.

Impact: Precise moment when the clubface and ball meet during the swing.

Intermediate target: Aiming point used to line up a shot to a target beyond the intermediate.

Iron: Clubs numbered from 1 to 9 and made in an assortment of wedges; the lower the number, the farther the ball travels.

Knee-knocker: Putt of short length, three to five feet.

Knock-down shot: Partial shot hit with low trajectory.

Lag: Putt struck from a long distance intended to stop within a few feet of the hole.

Lay-up shot: Playing a shot short of trouble, such as a water hazard.

Lie: (1) How the ball sits on the turf; (2) Current number of strokes played on a hole; (3) Angle the back of the clubshaft makes with the sole of the club.

Line of play: Direction the player wants the ball to travel, from where it lies to the hole.

Links: Traditional meaning is a course by the sea; modern usage is to use it to specify any golf course.

Lip: Edge of the hole or a bunker.

Lip out: Putt that rims or rolls along the edge of the hole.

Local rules: Additions to the Rules of Golf that are unique to a golf course.

Loft: Amount in degrees the clubface is angled.

> *If you think it's hard meeting new people, try picking up the wrong golf ball.*
> — *Jack Lemmon*

Long iron: Less-lofted clubs; the 1-, 2- and 3-irons.

Low handicapper: Usually an experienced player; a golfer who receives a low number of handicap strokes, such as under 10.

Low side: Area below the hole on a sloping putting green.

Match play: Tournament format in which one person or team competes against another person or team in a nine- or 18-hole match; the side that wins the most holes wins the match.

Medal play: Tournament format in which the strokes taken for a round determine the standings; professional medal play tournaments consist of three or four rounds; golfer with the lowest score wins. (Also called stroke play.)

Medalist: Lowest individual scorer in medal play (stroke) tournament.

Middle iron: The 4- 5- and 6-irons.

Mis-clubbed: Using the wrong club from what the shot required.

Mis-hit: Any shot that is not hit on the center of the clubface.

Mis-read: Not reading the correct amount of break on a putt.

Mixed foursome: Tournament format in which women and men compete simultaneously.

Mulligan: Hitting a second ball from the same spot as the first; usually given on the first tee; violates the Rules of Golf.

Nassau: Betting formula usually played for three points, one each for the front and back nines and one for the entire round, played in match play style.

Net score: Final score after a golfer's handicap has been applied to the gross score.

> *I'm hitting the woods just great, but I'm having a terrible time getting out of them.*
> — *Harry Toscanno*

Off-center hit: Shot hit on the perimeter of the clubface.

Off line: Shot hit away from the intended target.

Open tournament: Event that allows amateurs and professionals to compete at the same time.

Out-of-bounds: Course ground that is prohibited for play; hitting shots into these areas results in a penalty.

Overclub: Hitting a club that sends the ball farther than needed.

Overswing: Making too long of a backswing; swinging out of control.

Par: Score a good player would be expected to make on a hole, including two putts (such as a par 4); an 18-hole course usually has a par of 70 to 72.

Par-shooter: Golfer who makes mostly pars.

Penalty stroke(s): Must be added to score as the result of a violation of the Rules of Golf, such as hitting a ball out-of-bounds or into a water hazard.

GLOSSARY OF TERMS 103

Pin: See flagstick.

Pin high: See hole high.

Pitching: Playing short shots to the green with a wedge or high-lofted club.

Play through: Occurs when a faster group is allowed to pass a slower group.

Posture: Body position during the course of the swing.

Preferred lie: Allowing golfers to place the ball in an improved lie; usually ruled out during tournament play when weather has caused muddy conditions.

Preshot routine: Procedure performed in preparation to swing the club.

Press: (1) Hitting beyond a golfer's ability; (2) Betting game in which a losing team may double a bet on the final hole.

Professional: Golfer who plays the game for monetary compensation; usually a 0-handicapper or better.

Provisional ball: Hitting a second ball when the first is believed out-of-bounds or lost.

Pull: Shot that travels to the right of the target because of a swing flaw.

Punch shot: Shot with a lower than normal ball flight; usually played into the wind or under trees.

Push: Shot that travels to the left of the target because of a swing flaw.

Putt: One stroke taken on the putting green.

Putter: Club used to putt on the putting green, but can be used from surrounding short-cut grass.

Putting green: Area of very short-cut grass that surrounds the hole itself.

Quadruple bogey: Score on a hole four strokes more than par.

Recovery shot: Often risky; shot made to the fairway or green from a trouble area such as trees or thick rough.

Referee: Official accompanying a group to assist in rulings.

Rim: Ball that rolls over the edge of the hole; same as lip out.

Rough: Tall grass that borders the fairway and surrounds the green.

Round: Playing a complete set of holes, either nine or 18.

Rub of the green: Ball in flight accidentally stopped or deflected by an outside agency, such as a forecaddie.

Run: Ball that rolls a greater distance than normal.

Run-up shot: Playing shot short of the green and having it roll on.

Sandbag: Golfer who plays poorly on purpose to get a high handicap to use to his advantage in competition.

Scorecard: Card that lists hole pars and local rules and has space for player to write in his score.

Scratch player: Golfer of high skill; a 0-handicap.

Scuff: Hitting a thin shot; also, marking up a ball's cover.

Set up: Includes a golfer's posture, ball position during address.

Shaft: Usually metal but can be graphite or titanium; part of the club that connects the grip and clubhead.

Shank: Shot that flies to the left, caused by the swing flaw of the club hosel hitting the ball.

Short iron: The 7-, 8-, 9-irons and wedges.

Shot: Executing the swing.

Single: One golfer playing alone on the course.

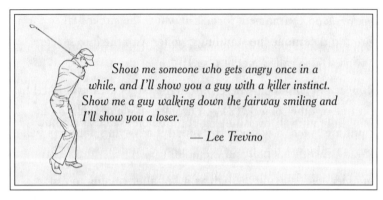

Show me someone who gets angry once in a while, and I'll show you a guy with a killer instinct. Show me a guy walking down the fairway smiling and I'll show you a loser.

— *Lee Trevino*

Skull: Hitting the top half of the ball because of a swing flaw; ball travels less than normal.

Sky: Hitting a ball much higher than normal.

Slice: Ball flight that sharply curves from right to left.

Snake: Putt made from a great distance with many breaks.

Snap hook: Ball flight that sharply curves from left to right, much more than a hook.

Sole: (1) Bottom portion of the club; (2) Letting the bottom of the club touch the ground at address.

Square: Having the feet, shoulders, knees, and elbows parallel to the ball-to-target line.

Staked trees: Newly planted trees that are tagged and held up by a stake; a local rule usually allows players to drop away from staked trees with no penalty.

Stance: Placement of the feet when swinging the club.

Stony: Shot hit very close to the flagstick; also called hitting the ball stiff.

Stroke: Either a full swing or putt made by the golfer with the intent of hitting the ball.

Stroke hole: Hole where a player receives a handicap stroke.

Stroke play: Tournament format in which the strokes taken for a round determine the standings; golfer with the lowest score wins. (Also called medal play.)

Stymie: (1) Situation where shot to the target area is blocked by a tree or other object; (2) An obsolete Rule of Golf; on the putting green, a golfer was stymied if a playing partner's ball was between his ball and the hole.

Summer golf: Playing the ball as it lies after coming to rest; playing by the official Rules of Golf.

Sweet spot: Usually the center of the clubface; the place on the clubface where the ball comes off most solid.

Swing: Actual movement made with a golf club to advance the ball forward.

> *My name used to be O'Connor, but I changed it for business reasons.*
> — Chi Chi Rodriguez

Swing length: Distance the golfer swings the club back on the backswing.

Swing plane: Imaginary "plane" that the golfer swings the club along; connects the shoulders and the ball.

Swing speed: How fast the club is moving at impact.

Swingweight: Golf club's weight distribution about a fixed fulcrum point. The higher the swingweight, the more the club feels heavy in the head.

Tailwind: Wind blowing from behind the golfer toward the target.

Take away: Initial stage of the swing from address until the hands reach hip height.

Target: Where the golfer intends the ball to finish.

Target line: Imaginary line from the ball to the target, used to help aim the club.

Target side: Side of the body or ball that is closest to the hole or target where the golfer is aimed.

Tee: (1) Short wooden or plastic peg used to hold the ball while teeing off; (2) Area of short grass from where a golfer begins play on a hole.

Tee markers: Used to indicate where golfers should play from on the tee.

Tee off: Playing a shot from the teeing ground.

Tee time: Assigned time for a group to begin play.

Teeing ground: Area of short grass from where play begins on a hole.

Tending the flag: Holding the flag while it is still in the hole for someone putting from a distant spot, then removing it after the ball is struck.

Texas wedge: Using a putter from off the green.

Thin shot: Similar to a bladed shot; striking the top half of the ball.

Threesome: Playing group of three players.

Through the green: Entire area of the course.

Toe: (1) Broad part of the clubface opposite where the shaft and clubhead join; (2) Swing flaw of hitting the ball on the toe.

Top: Swing flaw in which the club comes down directly on top of the ball.

Trajectory: Height and flight pattern of the ball after it's hit.

Trap: See bunker.

Triple bogey: Score on a hole three strokes more than par.

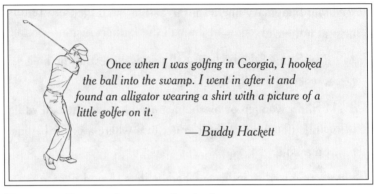

Once when I was golfing in Georgia, I hooked the ball into the swamp. I went in after it and found an alligator wearing a shirt with a picture of a little golfer on it.

— *Buddy Hackett*

Twosome: Group of two people playing.

Underclub: Using a club that doesn't hit the ball as far as needed.

Unplayable lie: Ball that rests in such a way that the player cannot make a swing at it; player takes a penalty stroke for moving the ball clear.

Up: Player leading a match.

Up and down: Occurs when player misses a green with his approach, but uses a chip shot and a putt to make a par.

Upright swing: Player's swing that is more vertical than normal.

Waggle: Short, back-and-forth movements with the club prior to the take away.

Wedge: High-lofted club used for short shots.

Weight shift: Body weight transferred from a centered position to the left side then centered and moved to the right during the swing for a left-handed player.

Whiff: Missing the ball completely while swinging; counts as a stroke.

Winter rules: Moving the ball six inches from its spot in the fairway, no closer to the hole; violates the Rules of Golf.

Woods: Clubs with wooden or metal heads, used for shots off the tee and fairway; woods hit the ball the farthest distances of all clubs.

Worm burner: A very low shot that scoots over the top of the grass.

Wrist cock: Hinging the wrists during the swing.

X'd out ball: Ball with an imperfection sold at a lower cost.

Yips: Muscle nervousness that adversely affects putting.

Glossary adapted from Youth Golf *by Cliff Schrock, published 1994 by Masters Press.*